ideals
FRIENDSHIP

Publisher, Patricia A. Pingry
Editor, Nancy J. Skarmeas
Art Director, Patrick McRae
Contributing Editors, Marty Sowder Brooks, Lansing Christman, Deana Deck, Russ Flint, Carol Shaw Johnston, Pamela Kennedy
Editorial Assistant, LaNita Kirby

ISBN 0-8249-1093-1

IDEALS—Vol. 48, No. 6 September MCMXCI IDEALS (ISSN 0019-137X) is published eight times a year: February, March, May, June, August, September, November, December by IDEALS PUBLISHING CORPORATION, P.O. Box 148000, Nashville, Tenn. 37214. Second-class postage paid at Nashville, Tennessee, and additional mailing offices. Copyright © MCMXCI by IDEALS PUBLISHING CORPORATION. POSTMASTER: Send address changes to Ideals, Post Office Box 148000, Nashville, Tenn. 37214-8000. All rights reserved. Title IDEALS registered U.S. Patent Office.

SINGLE ISSUE—$4.95
ONE-YEAR SUBSCRIPTION—eight consecutive issues as published—$19.95
TWO-YEAR SUBSCRIPTION—sixteen consecutive issues as published—$35.95
Outside U.S.A., add $6.00 per subscription year for postage and handling.

The cover and entire contents of IDEALS are fully protected by copyright and must not be reproduced in any manner whatsoever. Printed and bound in U.S.A.

ACKNOWLEDGMENTS

END OF SUMMER by Katherine Garrison Chapin. Used by permission of the estate; I AM STILL RICH from *HOME ROADS AND FAR HORIZONS* by Thomas Curtis Clark. Copyright © 1935 by Willett, Clark & Co. Reprinted by permission of HarperCollinsPublishers; UNHARVESTED from *THE POETRY OF ROBERT FROST* edited by Edward Connery Lathem. Copyright 1963 by Robert Frost. Copyright © 1964 by Lesley Frost Ballantine. Copyright © 1969 by Holt, Rinehart & Winston. Reprinted by permission of Henry Holt and Company, Inc.; THE MAKING OF A FRIEND from *THE PASSING THRONG* by Edgar A. Guest. © 1923 by the Reilly & Lee Co. Reprinted by permission of the estate; THROUGH PASTURE BARS from *NEW ENGLAND HERITAGE AND OTHER POEMS* by Rose Koralewsky. © 1949 by Bruce Humphries, Inc. Used by permission of Branden Publishing Company; SUNSHINE AND LAUGHTER by Otto Arthur Morton. Reprinted from *BEST LOVED UNITY POEMS*, first published by Unity School of Christianity, 1946; AUTUMN from *ALL ALONG THE WAY* by Isla Paschal Richardson. © 1922 by Bruce Humphries, Inc. Used by permission of Branden Publishing Company. Our sincere thanks to the following whose addresses we were unable to locate: Anne Campbell for TO MY FRIEND; Thomas Curtis Clark for FRIENDS; Strickland Gillilan for PARENTHOOD. Reprinted from the author's book *GILLILAN FINNIGAN AND COMPANY*; Sadie Stuart Hager for FRIENDSHIP from *EARTHBOUND.* © 1947 by Sadie Stuart Hager; Bertha Kleinman for FIND SOMETHING LOVELY from *THROUGH THE YEARS.* © 1957 by Bertha Kleinman; Leona Krefting for THE SWEETEST MUSIC IS IN KIND WORDS; May Smith White for AUTUMN'S MYSTERIOUS PATTERN; May Smith White for AUTUMN'S GOLDEN HOUR from *UPON RETURNING.* © 1958 by May Smith White; B. Y. Williams for THE FRIEND WHO JUST STANDS BY; Florence Rubert Wray for JOY'S SECRET.

Four-color separations by Rayson Films, Inc., Waukesha, Wisconsin
Printing by The Banta Company, Menasha, Wisconsin
The paper used in this publication meets the minimum requirements of American National Standard for Information Sciences—Permanence of Paper for Printed Library Materials, ANSI Z39.48-1984.

Unsolicited manuscripts will not be returned without a self-addressed stamped envelope.

Inside Covers, Frances Hook

Vol. 48, No. 6

Friends

Thomas Curtis Clark

If all the sorrows of the weary earth—
The pains and heartaches of humanity—
If all were gathered up and given me,
I still should have my share of wealth and worth
Who have you, friend of old, to be my cheer
Through life's uncertain fortunes, year by year.

Thank God for friends, who dearer grow
   as tears increase,
Who, as possessions fail our palsied hands,
Become the boon supreme, than gold and lands
More precious. Let all else, if must be, cease;
But Lord of Life, I pray, on me bestow
The gift of friends, to share the way I go.

The Friendly Type

Edna Jaques

The friendly type—how nice the phrase,
That someone has such happy ways,
A charm of manner, thought and speech,
The lonely folk of earth to reach.

The friendly type—oh, how we need
This kindliness of word and deed,
Of being able to express
The blessed warmth of friendliness,

Of putting strangers at their ease,
Of being happy when they please,
Whose inward happiness and grace
Are mirrored on a smiling face.

The friendly type—full-bosomed, sweet,
Whose laughter is a sort of treat,
That seems to kind of overflow,
And brings with it a special glow.

The friendly type—thank God for such,
Whose very presence holds a touch
Of the Divine—the blessed leaven,
That brings this old world nearer heaven.

Photo Opposite
HOME OF A FRIEND
Portsmouth, New Hampshire
Henry J. Hupp/Laatsch-Hupp Photo

Friendship

Sadie Stuart Hager

Friendship is a common,
    home grown flower,
But most uncommon are
    its growing ways;
Its seed can quicken,
    root within an hour,
Its lovely bloom survive
    the wintriest days.
It bears transplanting best
    when fully grown,
With roots fine-tendriled,
    spreading wide and deep;
Removed, it lives on memory
    soil alone—
A phantom field where cold
    winds ever sweep.
It is refreshed by fountains
    long gone dry,
This everlasting flower that
    will not die.

STONE BARN AT FRY'S HERB FARM
Manheim, Pennsylvania
Lefever/Grushow:
Grant Heilman Photography, Inc.

Photo Overleaf
COSMOS AND PUMPKINS
Route 7, Brandon, Vermont
Karen Wyle/H. Armstrong Roberts, Inc.

A Friend Like You

There's a joy that comes from sending
Wishes that are most sincere
For love and health and happiness
Each day throughout the year.

There's a joy that comes from hoping
All your fondest dreams come true—
Because it is so wonderful
To have a friend like you!

Patricia Mongeau
Munster, Indiana

To Have a Friend

To have a friend,
To know the joy of truly never being alone,
To share a thought, a day, a quiet moment,
    or a lifetime in the space of a heartbeat.

To have a friend:
I've got a problem—I'll listen.
I've run a little short—Here take mine.
I've got a good joke—Tell me.
My car broke down—Stay at my place.
I need a little help—Be right there.
I'm not very sleepy—Sit and talk a while.
I've got some friends coming to town—
    Good, bring them by for a cup of coffee.
I've got a good idea—Great, let's do it.
You sure are nice folks—Hush now, you talk
    too much.

Yes, maybe so,
But never enough to adequately say—
It's great to have a friend like you.

Gary Camp

Reflections

Just an Ordinary Somebody

The kettle is whistling in the kitchen,
Antique china so perfectly displayed;
Friendship is a noted priority,
Highlighted on my list today.
Napkins folded, silverware polished,
The cuckoo clock accurately chimes the time,
My heart leaps with such anticipation
For a friend is about to arrive.
The fresh aroma of buttermilk biscuits
Makes all seem cozy and sweet,
Tis a thrill to display my varied talents—
Add a friend to make the recipe complete.
A knock at the door is happily welcomed,
And I believe a wonderful day is here
'Cause a friend took precious moments
        to visit with me—
Just an ordinary somebody who cared.

Linda C. Grazulis
Pittsburgh, Pennsylvania

THROUGH PASTURE BARS

Rose Koralewsky

The drowsy hush of summer on the wane
Lies on the hillside pasture like a spell—
Enchantment that is only broken when
A slender, silver thread of melody
Embroiders on the air a faery tune.
Against a backdrop of unclouded blue
The pointed shapes of cedars darkly green
Rise from the sweetfern's lusty, fragrant growth
That carpets this long-neglected spot.

Around, a crumbling wall of lichened rock
Reveals itself behind a leafy screen
Where cherries hang in lustrous globes of jet.
Sunshine is everywhere; and like the sun,
The goldenrod its lavish treasure pours
Where later I shall hoard with jealous eye
A paltry branch or two of tarnished leaves.

Photo Opposite
WILDFLOWER MEADOW
Mendenhall, Pennsylvania
Larry Lefever/Grant Heilman Photography, Inc.

THROUGH PASTURE BARS

Rose Koralewsky

The drowsy hush of summer on the wane
Lies on the hillside pasture like a spell—
Enchantment that is only broken when
A slender, silver thread of melody
Embroiders on the air a faery tune.
Against a backdrop of unclouded blue
The pointed shapes of cedars darkly green
Rise from the sweetfern's lusty, fragrant growth
That carpets this long-neglected spot.

Around, a crumbling wall of lichened rock
Reveals itself behind a leafy screen
Where cherries hang in lustrous globes of jet.
Sunshine is everywhere; and like the sun,
The goldenrod its lavish treasure pours
Where later I shall hoard with jealous eye
A paltry branch or two of tarnished leaves.

Photo Opposite
WILDFLOWER MEADOW
Mendenhall, Pennsylvania
Larry Lefever/Grant Heilman Photography, Inc.

END OF SUMMER

Katherine Garrison Chapin

Summer is not ended
When a calendar page is turned, or when a few
Dry leaves fall whitened on green grass,
Or when the meadow spires
Ripen in amber fires,
Or early sky hangs cool above sea's change.
Summer has endings, unaware and strange,
Beyond bright days extended.

Summer is done
When no toys or rubbers lie below the steps,
An empty ladder leans against the barn,
Dogs bark at shadows, and their whines
Bring no whistled answer from the pines.
No screen doors bang; there is no
    admonitory hush
For sleep. Birds possess again the
    elderberry bush
Quietly, in the sun.

Summer was blended
Of laughter under trees, and shouts along
    a beach.
When the sands hold no print of quick bare feet,
No lithe and naked body of a child
Thigh-deep in minnows stares into the tide
(A fish-like being among fins and flippers)
And no one builds a wall against
    incoming waters,
Summer is ended.

SUMMER'S PASSING
New Harbour, Maine
Dick Dietrich, Photographer

CRUNCHY APPLE CRISP

4 cups peeled, sliced apples
½ cup water or apple juice
4 teaspoons firmly packed brown sugar
2 teaspoons lemon juice
¾ teaspoon cinnamon
2 tablespoons chopped almonds
½ cup oats
1 tablespoon firmly packed brown sugar
1 tablespoon margarine, melted

Heat oven to 375°. Combine apples, water, brown sugar, lemon juice, and cinnamon; toss lightly to coat apples. Arrange apples in an 8-inch square baking dish.

Combine remaining ingredients; mix well. Sprinkle over apples. Bake about 30 minutes or until apples are tender and topping is browned. Serve warm or chilled.

Nutrition Information

Serving Size: ¼ recipe

Calories	185	Sodium	37mg
Carbohydrates	32g	Calcium	34mg
Protein	3g	Cholesterol	0mg
Fat	6g	Dietary Fiber	3g

Recipe and photo courtesy of The Quaker Oats Company

September Gold

Anne Tilley

The liquid gold
Of summer sun
Drips through the trees
And sometimes runs
In rivulets
And often stands
In topaz puddles
In the sand.

September

LaVeta Stankovich

The woods flame red with scarlet oak
Or glow with poplar's burnished cloak.
Within a rustic garden gate,
Sweet pinks and cosmos blossom late;
The orchard boughs are bending low
Where ruddy yorks and pippens show.
Throughout each village, forest, farm
Steals gold September's peaceful charm.

FALL FUN
Cosmos, Minnesota
Bob Firth, Photographer

Sunshine and Laughter

Otto Arthur Morton

A laugh is just like music.
It lingers in the heart,
And where its melody is heard
The ills of life depart;

BEST FRIENDS
Robert Llewellyn/Superstock

And happy thoughts come crowding
   Its joyful notes to greet:
A laugh is just like music
   For making living sweet.

A laugh is just like the sunshine.
   It freshens all the day,
It tips the peak of life with light,
   And drives the clouds away.
The soul grows glad that hears it
   And feels its courage strong;
A laugh is just like sunshine
   For cheering folks along.

John Slobodnik

PARENTHOOD

Strickland Gillilan

Someone to snuggle up close to me there;
    Somebody's head on the thick of my arm;
Someone to help with her cuddle-time prayer;
    Someone believing I shield her from harm;
Somebody's dark-fearing hand I may hold
    Safe in my bigger one's sheltering keep;
Someone to guard till the morning light bold
    Rescues her eyes from the fetters of sleep!

Such are the yearnings that trouble us all
    After those wonderful babies have grown;
These are the hungers that tug and call
    After the nestlings have feathered and flown;
Only this heart's ease is comforting me,
    Missing my olden-time playfellow so:
She, in the years that shall presently be,
    Love like my love for herself shall know.

My Shadow

Robert Louis Stevenson

I have a little shadow that
    goes in and out with me,
And what can be the use of him
    is more than I can see.
He is very, very like me
    from the heels up to the head;
And I see him jump before me
    when I jump into my bed.

The funniest thing about him
    is the way he likes to grow—
Not at all like proper children,
    which is always very slow;
For he sometimes shoots up taller
    like an India-rubber ball,
And he sometimes gets so little
    that there's none of him at all.

He hasn't got a notion of
    how children ought to play,
And can only make a fool of
    me in every sort of way.
He stays so close beside me,
    he's a coward you can see;
I'd think shame to stick to nursie
    as that shadow sticks to me!

One morning, very early,
    before the sun was up,
I rose and found the shining dew
    on every buttercup;
But my lazy little shadow,
    like an errant sleepyhead,
He stayed at home behind me
    and was fast asleep in bed.

24

THROUGH MY WINDOW
— Pamela Kennedy —

THE PET TRAP

I have friends who confide in their dogs, commune with their cats, and chat with their parakeets. They enjoy a true comradeship with the animal kingdom. At Christmas, they hang up stockings for their pets and fill them with treats from the "Gourmet Pet Shoppe." I, on the other hand, am not a pet person. I enjoy little critters, but feel they ought to know their place—in zoos, trees, or burrows, or on old television shows like *Lassie* and *Fury* and *Rin-Tin-Tin.*

This anti-pet philosophy of mine was unopposed for years, until our children became old enough to determine that our home was lacking an essential component—animal friends. Then the campaign began. "Just a little pet, Mom." "We could get something that is no trouble!" (I defy anyone to show me a pet that is no trouble.)

Weakened by whines, I let my guard drop a bit. Our first pet was a snail, captured in the garden as he munched away his last moments of freedom on a chrysanthemum leaf. Simon the Snail lived in a Ball jar on my son's dresser for a few months, poorly disguised as a "science experiment." All he (or she) ever did was consume romaine leaves and create slimy patterns on the glass.

"Snails are basically boring," announced my seven-year-old as he dumped Simon back into the flower bed. "What we need around here is a real pet. " I disagreed, but the next week was the school carnival, and my daughter won a goldfish at the dart booth. I was positive Goldie wouldn't last a week, but she hung on for months, swimming endless circles in a glass mixing bowl. When Goldie finally turned belly-up, my tenderhearted daughter couldn't bear to bury her in a garden plot. Instead, she insisted we place the dead fish in the freezer in a tiny plastic bag, "Where I can visit her anytime I want!" The "orange anchovy"—as my husband insists upon calling it—still resides in the freezer and is dragged out on occasion for viewing by an incredulous visitor.

When the school guinea pig finished its rounds of fifth-grade classes, the teacher held a lottery to see who would win the honor of permanently adopting "Midnight."

"Oh, let him put his name in the hat," my soft-hearted mate urged, "what are the chances our son will win?"

Two days later, Midnight, a two-foot square cage, a month's supply of food pellets, and twenty-five pounds of cedar chips arrived at our house. "I promise to take care of him, Mom! You won't even know he's around!" Right.

It was all a lie. After the second week, the glamour of cleaning guinea pig droppings paled, and hunting for Midnight, who had a habit of scurrying under beds and large appliances, became a trial.

When we had our annual garage sale, Midnight went on the block. After several price reductions, he was carted off by a grinning, freckle-faced boy, who followed his uncertain mother down the driveway, chanting, "I promise to take care of him, Mom! You won't even know he's around!"

Our family remained petless for years after Midnight's departure and I, for one, did not grieve. But when our eldest, a throw-back to Dr. Doolittle, turned fifteen, we decided to grant his heart's desire and give him a kitten. With severe reservations, I brought home Ebony, a coal black ball of fur with golden eyes.

The kitten was cheap, but then there were the accessories: litter box, litter, food, dishes, flea comb, catnip mouse, shots, etc., etc., etc. My son was thrilled, however, and vowed to carefully tend to all of the kitten's needs—except, of course, when he had other things to do.

Ebony has lived at our house for a year now. She has delighted the children and driven me to distraction. I have replaced two shower curtains and thrown out several rolls of shredded toilet tissue. She has sharpened her claws on my husband's recliner and left it perforated in many places. My family room couch bears the scars of her attacks, as does my arm. (How was I to know that you shouldn't dry a wet cat with a blow dryer?) We can no longer defrost meat on the counter or leave the dinner dishes while we enjoy a second cup of coffee. She has claimed all the windowsills, cubby holes, cabinet tops, and corners as her own.

She has tried, in her feline way, to make friends with me by parading between my legs as I fix breakfast or curling up in my lap as I read a book. But I will not be taken in by her poorly disguised flattery. Even now, as I write this, she is stretched out on the windowsill, purring contentedly in a puddle of sunshine. She opens her golden eyes, blinks with mock innocence, and gazes at me seductively. She doesn't fool me, however. Her little cat brain is probably busy plotting her next terrorist attack on the furniture. She can purr all she wants; my heart will not be entered by little cat feet. And if she thinks she's getting another catnip mouse in her stocking next Christmas, she is sadly mistaken!

Pamela Kennedy is a freelance writer of short stories, articles, essays, and children's books. Mother of three children, she is married to a naval officer and has made her home on both U.S. coasts. She currently resides in Hawaii and draws her material from her own experiences and memories, adding bits of imagination to create a story or mood.

Find Something Lovely

Bertha Kleinman

Find something lovely every day you live,
And as you find it pass its beauty on,
For nothing prospers that you cannot give,
Nor thrives at best you cannot pass along.
Find something noble, every friend you meet,
Some lofty trait, perhaps a hidden one—
Something that you can make the more complete
When told to others what your friend has done;
Find something worth the while, no matter where,
At home, abroad, wherever you may go,
Some lovely bit of Truth—it's always there,
And when you find it let some other know;
Something ideal in sunshine or in rain,
That waits your touch to make it live again.

COLLECTOR'S CORNER

POSTCARDS

Postcards are a familiar part of our lives. We send them religiously when we are on vacation, announcing our latest travels to friends and family at home; and we receive them gladly also, posting their scenes of beautiful beaches and foreign wonders on the refrigerator as proof of our connection with the well-traveled. It is only natural, then, that postcards are one of the most popular collectibles.

Postcards were first printed in Austria in 1869, the creation of a German man named Emmanuel Herrman. They became an immediate success as an economical way of sending messages. Within three years, their popularity had spread throughout Europe and across the Atlantic to the United States. These early postcards—those printed up until 1898—are called "pioneer" cards.

It didn't take long for people to recognize the postcard's value as a collectible, and the interest of collectors further boosted the cards' already widespread appeal. Naturally, with the increase in popularity, publishers rushed to develop new themes and styles. The Colombian Exposition of 1892 to 1893 helped solidify the postcard's status as a collectible with its countless souvenir cards of Expo scenes, transportation themes, animals, birds, and advertising messages.

By the beginning of World War I, the use of postcards as a means of correspondence began to dwindle. They continued, however, to be much sought after by collectors. Today, as a paper collectible, they rank second only to stamps.

Although cards from the years 1898 to 1918 garner the most interest among collectors, the increasing cost of most of these cards has helped to turn collector's interest to cards from the 1920s, 1930s, and 1940s. Art Deco cards from the 1920s have gained a particularly devoted following.

Postcards from the collection of Robert Flanagan, New Rochelle, New York

General styles of postcards have evolved over the years. During the 1940s, cards with a textured, linen-like paper surface were produced. Later on, between 1950 and 1970, cards made on paper with a glossy surface became most popular.

Collectors are advised to concentrate on a single subject area, illustrator, or publisher. The two major categories of cards are view cards and topic cards. Whenever possible, cards for a collection should be in mint condition. There should be no creases, no writing on the picture side of the card, no dirt, no tears, and no sign of edge wear. Each of these defects can reduce the value by as much as ten percent. Stamps and cancellation marks, however, rarely affect the value of a card.

Although it might make sense that older cards would be more valuable, this isn't always the case. All collectibles, including postcards, are governed by the law of supply and demand. Thus, a more common postcard from the early 1900s might cost less than a rare card from the 1950s.

Flea markets, antique stores, garage sales, and grandma's attic can provide a wide variety of cards from which to begin or add to a collection. But certainly the most common way that a postcard collection begins is with the accumulation of cards sent to us by friends, or those bought as souvenirs of our own travels, for these are the cards that hold everlasting value in their ability to evoke our fond memories.

Carol Shaw Johnston, a public school teacher, writes articles and short stories. She lives with her family in Brentwood, Tennessee.

VERMONT WELCOME
Jamaica, Vermont
Barbara Laatsch-Hupp/Laatsch-Hupp Photo

DOORS

Edna Jaques

A door can be so wonderful;
    Crossing its threshold, I may see
Into another world,

Wide vistas opening up for me,
New work laid out, perhaps a friend,
New shining fields of life to tend.

NANTUCKET WELCOME
Nantucket, Massachusetts
Barbara Laatsch-Hupp/Laatsch-Hupp Photo

I love a doorway arched and old
　　With ivy creeping o'er the sill,
Great hinges wrought in hammered brass;
　　A knocker lying mute until
I lift its weight and let it fall,
　　Sending small echoes through the hall.

A little doorway, too, that leads
　　Only to warm enchanted places,
Firelight on a crimson rug,

A little group of happy faces
Joining in merry jest and play,
　　In the quiet evening of the day.

After the journey's length to find
　　A lighted doorway, half ajar,
The glow of candles shining out
　　Beside the doorway like a bar.
Across a thousand miles I see
　　A doorway beckoning to me.

BITS & PIECES

Lord, make me an instrument of your peace; where there is hatred, let me sow love; where there is injury, pardon; where there is doubt, faith; where there is despair, hope; where there is darkness, light; and where there is sadness, joy.

O Divine Master, grant that I may not so much seek to be consoled as to console; to be understood as to understand; to be loved as to love; for it is in giving that we receive, it is in pardoning that we are pardoned, and it is in dying that we are born to eternal life.

St. Francis of Assissi

He that does good to another does good also to himself, not only in consequence, but in the very act. For the consciousness of well-doing is in itself ample reward.

Seneca

Those who love not their fellow beings live unfruitful lives.

Percy Bysshe Shelley

34

Therefore all things whatsoever you would that men should do to you, do ye even so to them.

Matthew 7:12

Without friends, the world is but a wilderness. There is no man that imparteth his joys to his friends, but he joyeth the more; and no man that imparteth his griefs to his friends, but he grieveth less.

Francis Bacon

So long as we love, we serve; so long as we are loved by others, I should say that we are almost indispensable; and no man is useless while he has a friend.

Robert Louis Stevenson

Let all bitterness, and wrath, and anger, and clamor, and evil speaking be put away from you, with all malice.

Ephesians 4:31

That best portion of a good man's life,—
His little, nameless, unremembered acts
Of kindness and love.

William Wordsworth

The duty of man is not a wilderness of turnpike gates, through which he is to pass by tickets from one to the other. It is plain and simple and consists but of two points—his duty to God, which every man must feel; and, with respect to his neighbor, to do as he would be done by.

Thomas Paine

The Friend Who Just Stands By

B. Y. Williams

When trouble comes your soul to try,
You love the friend who just "stands by."
Perhaps there's nothing he can do—
The thing is strictly up to you;
For there are troubles all your own,
And paths the soul must tread alone;
Times when love cannot smooth the road
Nor friendship lift the heavy load,
But just to know you have a friend
Who will "stand by" until the end,
Whose sympathy through all endures,
Whose warm handclasp is always yours—
It helps, someway, to pull you through,
Although there's nothing he can do.
And so with fervent heart you cry,
"God bless the friend who just 'stands by.'"

Eleanor Roosevelt and Louis Howe:
A Useful Friendship

Eleanor Roosevelt was not entirely com-
fortable on board her husband's 1920
vice-presidential campaign train. The days
were long and the living quarters cramped and
spartan. Although she had longed for years to be
involved in her husband's political life, on the
train Eleanor felt out of place and isolated from
the purposes of the campaign. By day, Franklin
gave speeches, shook hands with voters, and con-
ferred with advisers; in the evenings he planned

strategy and played poker with the other men at the back of the train. Eleanor felt of little use.

Also aboard that train was Louis Howe, Franklin Roosevelt's campaign manager and friend. For years, Louis had been a frequent guest at the Roosevelt home; and while Franklin had always welcomed his friend, Eleanor had merely tolerated him. Howe had a brilliant political mind and was devoted to the advancement of Franklin's career; but he was a small, unsightly man, and his disheveled appearance and rough manner disturbed Eleanor's sense of reserve and propriety.

Connected only through Franklin, the two existed in different worlds. Eleanor lived a private, domestic life with her five children. Howe immersed himself in politics, particularly the politics of Franklin Delano Roosevelt. Their worlds intersected, but never truly touched each other. Not until the 1920 campaign, when circumstances gave Louis Howe a chance to see the quiet, dedicated intelligence of Eleanor Roosevelt, did Eleanor learn that beneath the rough exterior of Louis Howe was a true friend.

Eleanor Roosevelt—thirty-five years old and unaccustomed to life away from her home and family—was ready for a friend in her life. With five children to care for, a husband consumed by his own political ambitions, and a domineering mother-in-law reluctant to relinquish control of any aspect of family life to her son's wife, Eleanor had little encouragement to indulge her own growing interest in politics and public life. But the interest was sincere and strong, and she had boarded the campaign train full of hope for a new chapter in her life, if perhaps a bit troubled by self-doubt in the face of the unfamiliar.

Louis Howe was, on the exterior, exactly the man that Eleanor Roosevelt saw—a chain-smoking, untidy, unrefined man. But he was also a man of great sensitivity and insight. Howe sensed Eleanor's discomfort and loneliness; he saw that she lacked confidence in her public self. What he also saw were her intelligence and her good judgment. On the campaign trail that year he appealed to these traits. He brought Eleanor drafts of her husband's speeches and asked for her opinions. He looked to her for guidance on the "women's viewpoint," so important in 1920, the first year of the vote for women. He not only included her in

the business of her husband's campaign, he gave her a voice of her own.

When the campaign was over, Franklin had lost the election, but Eleanor had gained an ally; no more was Howe simply rough or unsightly, he was a friend. In the years that followed, Eleanor emerged as a public figure in her own right; and every step of the way, Louis Howe was there. He encouraged her interest in politics—not simply as the wife of a politician, but as an influential, individual voice. He coached her in public speaking, served as her literary agent, and taught her the practical skills of newspaper publishing.

Such encouragement, apparently, was all that Eleanor needed. When her husband was stricken with polio in 1921, she picked up the slack, keeping the Roosevelt name alive in New York politics. She became a leader in the League of Women Voters, the Women's Trade Union, the Leslie Commission, and the New York Democratic State Committee. She gave radio addresses, wrote articles and editorials, and was active in the fight for women's rights. She became, in other words, the Eleanor Roosevelt who is admired and emulated today, a woman of strength and grace with an unfailing commitment to public service.

Louis Howe was a part of Eleanor's life for the remainder of his own life. When Franklin was elected President, Eleanor experienced a return of the old self-doubts; she worried that her usefulness would be destroyed by her role as first lady. Howe, as always, had no doubts. In fact, without the least bit of condescension, he assured Eleanor that not only could she be first lady, she could be president. He believed in her and never allowed her to lose her belief in herself.

Eleanor Roosevelt once told an interviewer that the most honored goal one could pursue was the "privilege of being useful." Louis Howe gave her the confidence she needed to become useful and, through his commitment to his friend, proved his own usefulness. We can ask no better standard in choosing our own friends than that set by Eleanor Roosevelt and Louis Howe. Their friendship is proof that our greatest friends do more than simply mirror back to us the person that they see, rather they see beyond the present to the person we can become.

Campobello Island

LIGHTHOUSE AT CAMPOBELLO
New Brunswick, Canada
Dick Dietrich Photography

Campobello Island is a unique symbol of a friendship between two neighboring nations—a monument to a great American president located on Canadian soil and administered and funded through the cooperative efforts of both countries.

Franklin Delano Roosevelt referred to Campobello Island simply as "my beloved island." For the President and the members of his family, Campobello—located in the Bay of Fundy in New Brunswick, Canada, only miles by bridge from the state of Maine—was a cherished retreat, second in their affections only to their New York home at Hyde Park. From 1883, when he was only a year old, until 1921, when he was stricken by polio, Franklin spent nearly every summer on

the island. First with his parents, James and Sara, and later with Eleanor and their five children, Roosevelt found an escape from the pressures of public life on Campobello, sailing and swimming in Lake Glen Severn and in the clear, cold waters of the Bay of Fundy, and hiking along the miles of beautiful, unspoiled cliffs and beaches.

Franklin and Eleanor made their summer home in a wonderful thirty-four room "cottage" on the island's western shore, overlooking Friar's Bay to Eastport, Maine. The cottage was a wedding gift from Franklin's mother, Sara Delano Roosevelt, and it quickly became a second home to Eleanor, Franklin, and their growing family. In later years, Franklin's polio and the demands of his presidency would limit the time he spent on the island; but the Roosevelts never lost touch with Campobello, returning as often as possible to the scene of so many of their happiest memories.

Today, the Roosevelt cottage remains, along with four others built by wealthy American families around the turn of the century. All are now part of Roosevelt Campobello International Park. Established in 1964 by an agreement between President Lyndon Johnson of the United States and Prime Minister Lester B. Pearson of Canada, the park is the only one of its kind in the world. Located within the borders of New Brunswick, the park is funded and administered by a committee made up of both Americans and Canadians.

The Roosevelt cottage has been restored, recreating the summer home that was a haven to Franklin and Eleanor. The President's office, Eleanor's writing room, and several family rooms are filled with the Roosevelt's furniture, papers, and mementos. The cottage also houses an extensive collection of Franklin Delano Roosevelt's memorabilia, including pictures and papers from his childhood, family life, and years in public office. The Park offers tours of the cottage, along with a short film that describes the longstanding affection of the Roosevelt family

for their beloved Campobello. The other four cottages on the island have also been restored and are used as guest houses for travelers and as residences for the island's many professional and academic conferences.

The beaches and cliffs and woodlands that the Roosevelts loved are now protected park land, accessible to the public year round. Over two and a half thousand acres of shoreline, forest, cliffs, and open fields, all accessible by well-maintained walking trails and scenic drives, cover the island, which is a sanctuary to thousands of shore birds and other migrating species.

Campobello, with its breathtaking ocean views and cool sea breezes, is a beautiful, serene spot—it is not difficult to imagine a young FDR and his family sailing off its shores or picnicking on its beaches. But the island today is more than a memorial to a single individual or family, it is a tribute to a friendship between two great nations. On Campobello Island, the United States and Canada come together in common recognition of our longstanding political and cultural ties and in celebration of the precious natural resources that we share.

ROOSEVELT COTTAGE
Campobello Island, New Brunswick, Canada
Dick Dietrich Photography

A SLICE OF LIFE

Edgar A. Guest

The Making of a Friend

We nodded as we passed each day
    And smiled and went along our way;
I knew his name, and he knew mine,

But neither of us made a sign
    That we possessed a common tie;
    We barely spoke as we passed by.

How fine he was I never guessed.
    The splendid soul within his breast
I never saw. From me were hid
    The many kindly deeds he did.
His gentle ways I didn't know,
    Or I'd have claimed him long ago.

Then trouble came to me one day,
    And he was first to come and say
The cheering words I longed to hear.

He offered help, and standing near
I felt our lives in sorrow blend—
    My neighbor had become my friend.

How many smiles from day to day
    I've missed along my narrow way;
How many kindly words I've lost,
    What joy has my indifference cost?
This glorious friend that now I know,
    Would have been friendly years ago.

Edgar A. Guest began his illustrious career in 1895 at the age of fourteen when his work first appeared in the Detroit Free Press. *His column was syndicated in over 300 newspapers, and he became known as "The Poet of the People."*

Friendship

Corinne Roosevelt Robinson

Though love be deeper,
    friendship is more wide;
Like some long road stretching limitless,
It may not feel the ultimate caress
Of sun-kissed peaks, remote and glorified,
But here the light with gentle winds allied
The broad horizon sweeps, till loneliness,
The cruel tyrant of the soul's distress,
In such sweet company may not abide.

Friendship has vision, though
    dear love be blind,
And swift and full communion in the fair
Free flight of high and sudden ecstasy,
The broad excursions where, mind
    knit to mind,
The heart renewed can all things dare,
Lit by the fire of perfect sympathy.

COUNTRY ROAD
Orford, New Hampshire
Dick Dietrich, Photographer

A Year of Short Wave Cheer: Friendship Bridge to Britain

Five nights a week between 9-9:30 p.m., English daylight time, war-harried Britons, often huddled in air-raid shelters, tune in on an American radio program which for months has been bringing them moral encouragement and cheer. On Tuesdays, it warms their hearts with the voices of British refugee children prattling messages to kinfolk, and on Mondays, Wednesdays, Thursdays, and Fridays, it diverts them with a variety, dramatic, or musical show, or a timely talk.

Headliners ranging from Albert Einstein to Al Schacht, baseball clown, have contributed these bits for Britain, all gratis. Eleanor Roosevelt participated in a South African program; Metropolitan Opera singers joined in an all-Anzac revue, and Eddie Cantor sizzled the air waves with peppery bon mots.

This program, aptly named Friendship Bridge, was thought up by Walter S. Lemmon, distinguished New York radio engineer and president of the World Wide Broadcasting Foundation, which operates the Boston short-wave station WRUL. Last August, when the air blitz opened, Lemmon mused: "I have an aerial bridge to Britain in WRUL—what can I do to help?" He talked to William V. C. Ruxton, head of British American Ambulance Corps, and Donald Flamm, then owner of station WMCA, New York, and a week later Friendship Bridge, a project of all three, was spanning the ocean, with three broadcasts emanating from WMCA and two from WRUL, and all short-waved by the Boston station.

Marking a year's operations, Friendship Bridge last week staged an anniversary broadcast and a party at WMCA studios. Present were Lemmon, Edward J. Noble, the Life Savers candy man who now owns WMCA, Raymond G. Swing, who introduced the original program, and Sir Gerald Campbell, British information chief here. Fittingly enough, the milestone was observed on a child-refugee program, most popular of the broadcasts.

To date, more than 500 of these blitz fugitives have sat around a table above roaring Broadway to read scrawled notes to home folk. Once, a little tyke insisted that he was the Lone Ranger. On another program, two Scotch youngsters staying in the South confessed that they had swapped their burrs for drawls. A boy once asked his dad to keep his bike greased, and several shavers have complained that American history books are all wrong.

Parents and friends cannot reply to children as in a two-way conversation program broadcast monthly by NBC. But that they and multitudes of others do listen in is testified by countless letters. A sample excerpt from a letter: "I write this by light of a torch held under a blanket. It is good to know that you are thinking of us while the bombs are thudding all around."

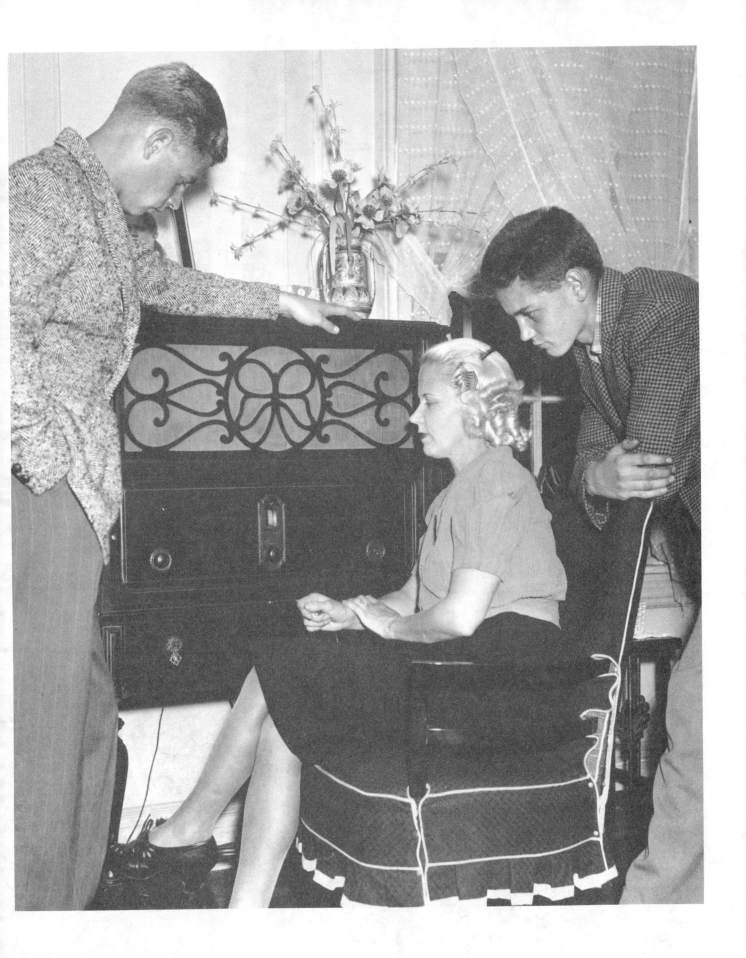

To My Friend

Anne Campbell

I have never been rich before,
But you have poured
Into my heart's high door
A golden hoard.

My wealth is the vision shared,
The sympathy,
The feat of the soul prepared
By you for me.

Together we wander through
The wooded ways.
Old beauties are green and new
Seen through your gaze.

I look for no greater prize
Than your soft voice.
The steadiness of your eyes
Is my heart's choice.

I have never been rich before,
But divine
Your step on my sunlit floor
And wealth is mine!

Photo Opposite
HARVEST WAGON AT CHAPLIN'S CABINS
Naples, Maine
Dick Dietrich, Photographer

The Sweetest Music Is in Kind Words

Leona Krefting

Not in great orchestrations,
Nor in hymns sung clear and sweet,
Nor in anthems chanted in chords
That over and over repeat;

Not in the songs of thousands,
But in one kindly word
From the lips of a gentle fellow man
Is the sweetest music ever heard.

In times of sorrow, peace is brought
By kind words softly spoken,
And joy is shared in happy ways
With friendship's chain unbroken.

The gentle words, the kindly words,
Bring peace to troubled mind,
And the sweetest music ever heard
Is in words soft and kind.

I Am Still Rich

Thomas Curtis Clark

I am still rich.
The morning comes with old-time cheer;
    The sun breaks through the blurring mist;
And all the sorrows of the night
    By newborn rays of hope are kissed.
Up and rejoice! a spirit cries,
What is your loss, with morning skies!

I am still rich.
My friends are faithful, as of old;
    They trust me past my poor desert.
They ask no gift of golden grain,
    But only love. With their strength girt,
Can I not face the road ahead—
Though some old treasured joys are dead!

I am still rich.
I have my work, which constant calls;
    I could not loiter, if I would;
Each moment has some task to speed,
    Some work to do. How kind, how good,
Is life that God now grants to me—
A segment of Eternity!

Photo Opposite
ROADSIDE MARKET
Stevens, Pennsylvania
Larry Lefever/Grant Heilman Photography, Inc.

The Making
of
Friends

Author Unknown

If nobody smiled and nobody cheered
And nobody helped us along,
If each person only looked after himself,
And all good things went to the strong;

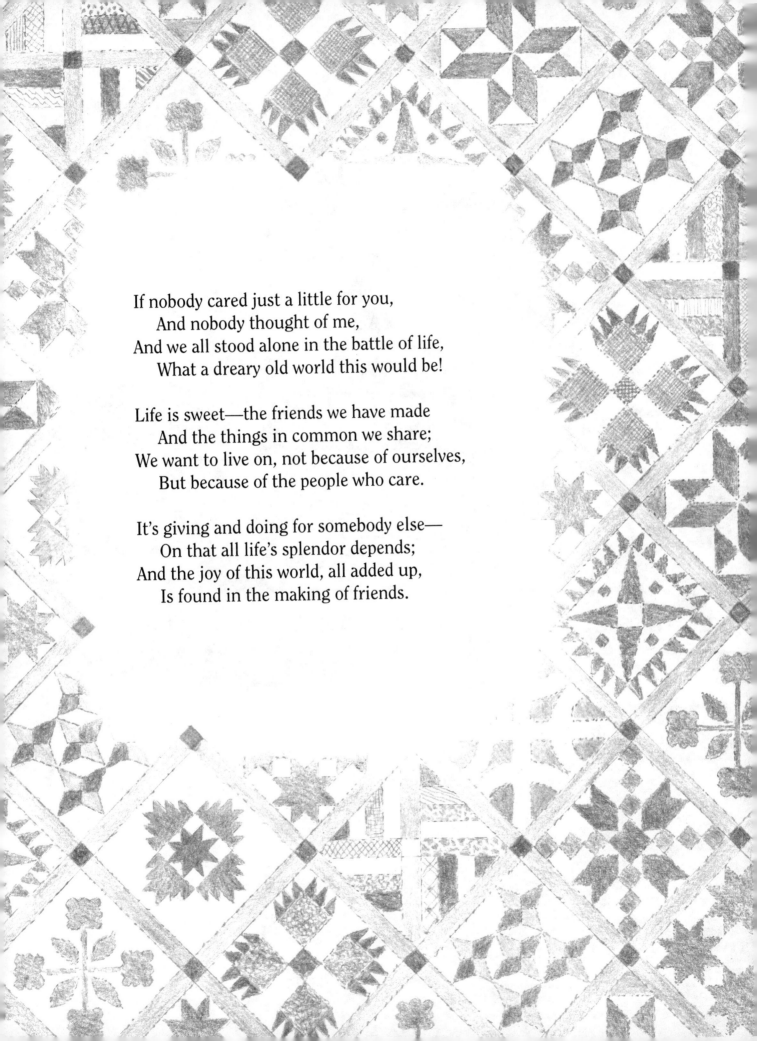

If nobody cared just a little for you,
    And nobody thought of me,
And we all stood alone in the battle of life,
    What a dreary old world this would be!

Life is sweet—the friends we have made
    And the things in common we share;
We want to live on, not because of ourselves,
    But because of the people who care.

It's giving and doing for somebody else—
    On that all life's splendor depends;
And the joy of this world, all added up,
    Is found in the making of friends.

Old Friends Are Precious Things

June Masters Bacher

Why was it in my youth that I
Made plans to walk away
From places, faces that I loved
In that dear yesterday?
I did not know the pain that comes
From putting on the new,
Or that those dear, old, trusted friends
Are very, very few.

I dreamed of Cinderella gowns
When I was but a lass,
And rushed away one magic day
In slippers made of glass.
Ah, yes, they shattered
When I dashed
My foot against a stone;
And life has split my heart in half—
Of course, I should have known.
For old friends are a precious thing
We should not leave behind;
And youth, not age, I've found at last,
Is, oh, my friends, so blind!

Photo Opposite
QUILT AUCTION
Manheim, Pennsylvania
Larry Lefever/Grant Heilman Photography, Inc.

I Know Not What the Future Hath

John Greenleaf Whittier

I know not what the future hath
    Of marvel or surprise,
Assured alone that life and death
    His mercy underlies.

And if my heart and flesh are weak
    To bear an untried pain,
The bruised reed He will not break,
    But strengthen and sustain.

No offering of my own I have,
    Nor works my faith to prove;
I can but give the gifts He gave
    And plead His love for love.

And so beside the silent seas
    I wait the muffled oar;
No harm from Him can come to me
    On ocean or on shore.

I know not where His islands lift
    Their fronded palms in air;
I only know I cannot drift
    Beyond His love and care.

Who Bides His Time

James Whitcomb Riley

Who bides his time, and day by day
Faces defeat full patiently,
And lifts a mirthful roundelay,
However poor his fortunes be,
He will not fail in any qualm
Of poverty—the paltry dime
It will grow golden in his palm,
    Who bides his time.

Who bides his time—he tastes the sweet
Of honey in the saltiest tear;
And though he fares, with slowest feet,
Joy runs to meet him, drawing near;
The birds are herald of his cause;
And like a never-ending rhyme,
The roadsides bloom in his applause,
    Who bides his time.

Who bides his time, and fevers not
In the hot race that none achieves,
Shall wear cool wreathen laurel, wrought
With crimson berries in the leaves;
And he shall reign a goodly king,
And sway his hand o'er every clime,
With peace writ on his signet ring,
    Who bides his time.

59

How Still, How Happy!

Emily Brontë

How still, how happy! Those are words
That once would scarce agree together;
I loved the plashing of the surge,
The changing heaven, the breezy weather,

More than the smooth seas
   and cloudless skies
And solemn, soothing, softened airs
That in the forest woke no sighs
And from green spray shook no tears.

How still, how happy! Now I feel
Where silence dwells is sweeter far
Than laughing mirth's most joyous swell
However pure its raptures are.

Come, sit down on this sunny stone;
'Tis wintry light o'er flowerless moors—
But sit—for we are all alone
And clear expand heaven's
   breathless shores.

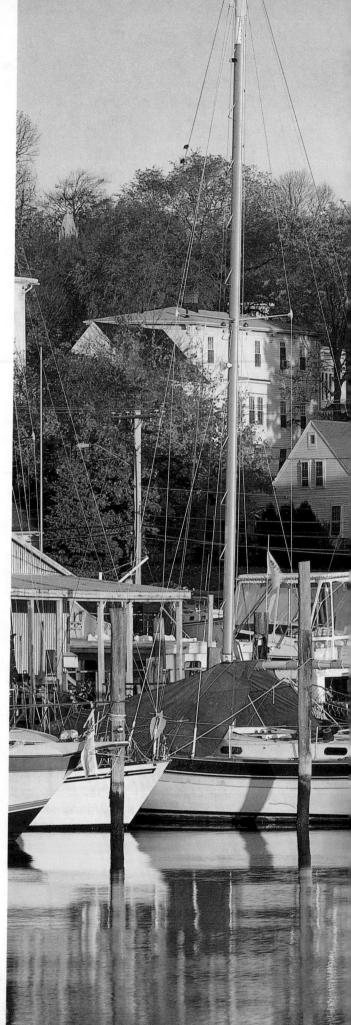

BOATS AND REFLECTIONS
Mystic, Connecticut
William Johnson/Johnson's Photography

Country CHRONICLE
—— Lansing Christman——

That nature which to one is a stark and ghastly solitude is a sweet, tender, genial society to another.

Henry David Thoreau

I long ago became a member of that genial society. I go often to the woods and open countryside, to pastures where cattle graze in bucolic settings of sun and shade that lead down the slopes to murmuring brooks. I find friends everywhere I go.

62

There are the birds, the trees and shrubs, and the animals. There are the crickets and the katydids, my instrumentalists, and my friends the wildflowers.

Come walk with me if you will. We will find friends at every turn—a chickadee or a song sparrow, a woodchuck or a chipmunk, an oak or a maple, the wild rose or the steeplebush.

I was just a boy when on a winter's day in the woods the chickadees began flitting about me, singing their sweet and tender song. I stood there, amazed and surprised, as still as I could be, listening and watching. Suddenly, the chickadees started to settle on my arms and shoulders. Right then and there I pledged to accept and protect as my friends all of God's creatures in the outdoor world. And ever since, our friendship has remained strong.

The author of two published books, Lansing Christman has been contributing to Ideals *for almost twenty years. Mr. Christman has also been published in several American, foreign, and braille anthologies. He lives in rural South Carolina.*

Unharvested

Robert Frost

A scent of ripeness from over a wall.
And come to leave the routine road
And look for what had made me stall,
There sure enough was an apple tree
That had eased itself of its summer load,
And of all but its trivial foliage free,
Now breathed as light as a lady's fan.
For there had been an apple fall
As complete as the apple had given man.
The ground was one circle of solid red.

May something go always unharvested!
May much stay out of our stated plan,
Apples or something forgotten and left,
So smelling their sweetness would be no theft.

FROM MY
G·A·R·D·E·N
JOURNAL

Deana Deck

DRYING FLOWERS

I love fresh flowers. I grow them in profusion, scatter them lavishly throughout the house, use them to celebrate even the smallest occasion, and usually keep some in the office to remind me of the real world. As a result, I have dozens of vases of every size and shape, and if I could, I would have them filled with fresh flowers year round.

The problem is that, sooner or later, my garden gives up the ghost for winter and, except for holiday plants and brave little African violets, the house is deprived of those joyful splashes of color that keep me happy from earliest spring into late fall.

That's when I turn to dried flowers. Out they come, from where they have been waiting in boxes of sand and silica and borax, from where they have been hanging in the attic, basement, and garage. After a minimum of preparation, colorful bouquets, accented with preserved foliage, once again grace every room.

A great many flowers can be dried simply by hanging them upside down in a dry, airy location. It makes sense to include a few of these varieties in your garden, even if you haven't the space or time available to create elaborate dried arrangements.

Statice, straw flowers, and baby's breath are probably the most commonly dried flowers, because they are easy to grow and they retain their shape and color when dried. Larkspur, globe amaranth, and yarrow are other easily grown and dried varieties.

Hydrangea, set upright in a vase with half an inch of water, makes a beautiful dried flower within a couple of weeks. All you do is let the water slowly evaporate. This method works well with baby's breath too, although it can also be hung to dry. To preserve the graceful curves of their foliage, most grasses are also dried standing upright.

Roses, zinnias, marigolds, daisies, asters, and even peony blooms can be successfully dried, but they need a little more help. These do best when dried in desiccates such as sand, silica, or borax, which pull the moisture away from the petals, leaving shape and color behind. The more delicate the bloom, the more effort it requires, but none are difficult.

You may want to experiment with various desiccates to find which one you prefer. Borax is available in the laundry soap section of the supermarket. It is extremely light, which makes it preferable for delicate blossoms, and it works in two to ten days, depending upon the flower. Its drawback is the powdery residue it leaves behind, which is difficult to remove from delicate petals and complicated flower heads. I use a camel's hair brush to remove the powder, but it is tedious and messy.

Silica gel, which has the consistency of finely granulated sugar, can be found in most hobby stores and at many florists. I prefer it for nearly every flower type. It is quick—completing most jobs in two or three days—and it leaves no powder behind. It is best for retaining clear, bright colors. It is also the most expensive desiccate, but has the advantage of being almost infinitely reusable.

Sand, finely grained, cleaned, and sifted, works a little slower than the others—taking anywhere from a week to a month—but it is very easy to obtain and ranges in price from inexpensive to free. It can be found in hardware stores, lumber yards, or at the beach. (Beach sand should be washed thoroughly to remove all salt, sifted to get rid of debris, and dried in a 300° oven to kill any microorganisms.)

Both sand and silica gel can be used in the microwave for the fastest results, but be sure to place a cup of water in the microwave to absorb energy. Dry from one to three minutes, then remove from the microwave and let stand for thirty-six hours without disturbing. This quick-dry method is wonderful for preserving colors, since they don't have time to fade.

Not all flowers do well in the microwave, but those that excel include tulips, carnations, peonies, pansies, roses, and mums. Be prepared to experiment at first, however, because each flower requires its own drying time.

Prepare flowers for drying by cutting off all but about a half inch of stem—leave just enough to hold on to. It is very important that the flowers be free of dew or other moisture before placing them into the container of desiccate, especially if you plan to use borax. The drying container should have a lid that is airtight, except when microwaving.

Flat blossoms, like daisies, asters, and cosmos, are dried face down in the desiccate. Place roses and other rounded, delicate blooms face up on a bed of desiccate and gradually fill in the spaces around the flower. Dribble the medium gently with your fingers or a spoon so as not to crush the petals with a sudden weight. Build up layers slowly to preserve the natural shape of the blossom.

After the bloom is dried, insert an artificial stem of wire (available at your florist) into the stub and then attach with green florist's tape. If the flower is heavy, use a "hairpin" technique to prevent slipping. Push one end of the wire up through the stem and the flower. Bend the wire at center and thread the end back through flower and stem. Wind florist's tape around the wire ends to create a natural-looking stem.

With the simplicity and versatility of dried flowers, there is no reason not to have the colors of the natural world in your home year round—even when Nature herself has turned brown and bare.

Deana Deck lives in Nashville, Tennessee, where her garden column is a regular feature in the Tennessean.

CRAFTWORKS

The beauty and fragrance of summertime blossoms need not vanish from your home each September. These two simple craft ideas—Pressed Flower Bookmarks and Potpourri-Filled Vases—preserve the color and scent of the summer for the long cold months ahead. Both make lovely gifts for friends or family—anyone who cherishes the beauty of the garden or the countryside.

Pressed Flower Bookmarks

Marjorie Kraus

Marjorie Kraus loves to take walks in the country around her Alum Bridge, West Virginia, home. These bookmarks are her way of preserving the beautiful wildflowers she finds along her walks, and sharing her love of nature with friends.

Materials Needed

    Fresh flowers
    White or ivory poster board
    Clear contact paper
    Ribbon (optional)

Gathering and Preparing Flowers

Marjorie uses the wildflowers native to her area—miniature pansies, buttercups, zinnias, cosmos, miniature hollyhocks—for her bookmarks, but nearly any flower will do. Dainty green leaves such as those from Queen Anne's lace, ground pine, or rock fern can also be pressed to provide accent to the flowers.

Once flowers are selected, they must be pressed while still fresh between two pieces of absorbent, non-glossy paper. Use heavy books to keep flat. Flowers and leaves take from two to three weeks to dry thoroughly.

Making Bookmark

Cut poster board into rectangles approximately seven inches high and three inches wide. Arrange dried flowers and leaves on the poster board, leaving at least one quarter inch between flowers and edges.

Once your arrangement is set, cover the bookmark with contact paper. Peel back an inch of the contact paper and press it slowly onto the poster board, about a half-inch at a time. Keep the flowers in place and smooth as you go. After the bookmark is covered, trim the edges of the contact paper so that they are even with the edge of the board.

For an extra touch of color, punch a hole in the bookmark about a quarter of an inch from the top in center. Thread an eight-inch length of ribbon, folded in half, through hole. Thread the two ends through the ribbon loop and pull tight.

Potpourri-Filled Vases

Marty Brooks

For these beautiful potpourri-filled vases, Marty Brooks uses simple materials available at any craft store. Potpourri comes in a variety of scents and colors; add a matching ribbon, and you have a wonderful, aromatic accent for any room.

Materials Needed

    Clear or lightly tinted glass vase
        with flared neck
    Potpourri
    Thread doily (at least 4 inches wider in
        diameter than top of vase.)
    Rubber band
    Ribbon

Fill the bowl of the vase with fragrant, colorful potpourri. Lay the doily on top of the vase and slip the rubber band over doily around neck of vase. Adjust the ruffles so that they spread evenly around neck. Cut a piece of ribbon long enough to wrap around neck and form a bow, covering rubber band.

Photo Opposite
Gerald Koser

MYSTERIOUS PATTERN

May Smith White

The day grew quiet here. No ripples played
Upon the austere sky. And golden leaves
Hung motionless, as if each one obeyed
The pattern set when browning autumn grieves.
But soon each leaf will yield itself to earth,
Weaving a russet carpet once again,
And autumn fires then will come to birth,
Quenched later by the cold November rain.

Here lie the mysteries that autumn keeps;
And through this time her songs will lull the heart
As plans grow richer, as all nature sleeps,
Because her deftness is her counterpart.
With changing seasons I still yearn to see
The sign of autumn in the maple tree.

AUTUMN

Isla Paschal Richardson

No, no, I must protest against the word
Too often given to this season—"sad."
All things need not be true that we have heard,
For autumn tries to tell us it is glad
Because there have been spring and summer blooms;
It now bedecks itself in colors, all
Rich royal bronze and red and gold costumes;
The trees and fields will take a curtain call
Before retiring for their winter sleep.

Yes, there is something vital in the air,
Impellent urge of praise, profound and deep,
As though Nature, lifting her head in prayer,
Recounts past blessings. Summer slips away,
And smiling whispers she'll be back some day.

Photo Overleaf
SILVER CASCADES OF
CRAWFORD NOTCH STATE PARK
Crawford Notch, New Hampshire
William Johnson/Johnson's Photography

Joy's Secret

Florence Rubert Wray

Farewell, summer! Joy turns and runs
With arms outstretched, to burnished suns
And vivid hills, to startling skies,
Grasping glory. The secret lies
Behind all this in that Joy knows
Soon color drowns in winter's snows.
Here, where this green or gold is flung,
Where crimson starts and blue is hung,
There will be nought but gray and white,
The paling tints of evening light,
Shadowed violet and stenciled black,

More somber tones that, silent, track—
Indian-like, in single file—
The trail of time and all the while
The world will wait, subdued and still.
Now, Joy must turn and take its fill
Of etchings—clear, sharp, fragile, fine—
Of beauty found in form and line,
Yet feel no need to color these
Slender-fingered, thin, black-boled trees,
Nor penciled ponds, nor frozen sky.
Warm when the winds go mourning by,
Content with hushed and dreaming things,
Joy hugs the hearth and softly sings,
Knowing within its heart of hearts,
Where beauty stops, new beauty starts.

Autumn's Golden Hour

May Smith White

Walk quietly here—
Lest birds be stirred to flight
By sound of feet
Upon the russet leaves
Along the garden path.

Walk slowly—
Lest you miss the beauty
Of this golden hour
That soon will purple
Beneath autumn skies.

Walk gently—
While life becomes imbued
With nature's riches,
And hopes that once were only dreams
Lie warm upon the heart.

RESTORED HOME AND SUGAR MAPLE
Mystic, Connecticut
William Johnson/Johnson's Photography

Readers' Forum

I am writing from a nursing home in Little Falls, Minnesota. I would like to compliment you on your beautiful magazine. We use it in our Reality Orientation program. Your beautiful colorful pictures bring fond memories of home to our residents. Your pictures and readings of "yesteryear" are fantastic. Keep up the good work. I am ordering the magazine for one of our residents who especially finds happiness in its pages!

June Shutter
Little Falls, Minnesota

Six-month-old Halen Howard shows his Fourth of July colors.

For years I have enjoyed Ideals Christmas. The pictures are so beautiful and the poems are read over and over again.

Our church Christmas program . . . was poems from past issues. We used appropriate music along with the poetry. Everyone said it was the best program yet.

It's good to know we can still purchase this quality of reading and art, all in one lovely book. Thank you for the pleasure you bring to many people with Ideals magazine

Nora A. Rensel
Palatka, Florida

Give Every Child a Flag

Give our children flags to wave
So that they will understand
Our country has a birthday
Celebrated throughout the land!

Let every little wisp of wind
Set those flags to wave
As freedom continues to fly
Over the land of the brave.

Give our children flags to hold—
Decoration tried and true;
Teach them well and early on
Love for the red and white and blue.

Starlette Howard
Ogden, Utah

78

When I received your offer for a free "Get Acquainted" issue of Ideals magazine, I certainly didn't expect anything like I received in the mail today. I've just glanced through it and find it just wonderful.

The Last Supper on the inside front cover is exactly what I have been looking for. We just renovated our kitchen and I was searching for a different picture of The Last Supper to fit in with our new look kitchen. I found an old frame in the attic and have cut it down to fit your print.

The pictures of the beautiful spring flowers gave a boost to my spirits, as the winter is long and cold here in the Adirondack Mountains. I know I am also going to enjoy the poems and stories.

Mary H. Condra
Blue Mountain Lake, New York

This picture was taken in a hanging plant on my front porch this summer. A robin built her nest within a week after hanging this plant up. All four eggs hatched and I got to see them fly away. I've seen your magazine and thought if you could use this picture in some way you are welcome to do so.

Evelyn Pyzik
Anderson, Indiana

Please send me another copy of Ideals Easter, Volume 48, No. 2. My friend fell in love with George Hinke's The Last Supper and He Is Risen. I am not about to give up my copy.

Mable Riley
Sedalia, Missouri

Editor's Note: Readers are invited to submit unpublished, original poetry, short anecdotes, and humorous reflections on life for possible publication in future Ideals issues. Please send copies only; manuscripts will not be returned. Writers receive $10 for each published submission. Send material to: "Readers' Reflections," Ideals Publishing Corporation, P.O. Box 140300, Nashville, TN 37214-0300.